We Need to Talk About Edu

We Need to Talk About Education

We Need to Talk About Education

Dreams, aspirations and realities of a generation

Ben Faccini   Greg Villalobos

We Need to Talk About Education:
Dreams, aspirations and realities of a generation
Original writing by Ben Faccini
Images by Greg Villalobos

Copyright © 2014 Ben Faccini and Greg Villalobos
ISBN: 978-1-908041-18-0
Published by IndieBooks Limited,
4 Staple Inn, London WC1V 7QH
www.indiebooks.co.uk

Printed by Butler Tanner and Dennis Limited,
Caxton Road, Frome, Somerset BA11 1NF
Set in Calluna
Printed on FSC certified paper
1 3 5 7 9 8 6 4 2

Contents

Preface

I began my journey through education as a pupil on free school meals in an underfunded state school in a deprived borough of London. I came from a working-class background, neither of my parents went to university, and my mother worked in a factory during the day before putting in a night shift at the local McDonalds. Statistically, it was highly unlikely that I would go on to achieve the things I have accomplished since leaving school, but the support of many teachers and the stability of my family helped get me there. The challenges described by the young people who have contributed to this book are very familiar to those from my own time at school.

In Year 10, I didn't have one English teacher, I had six – a new supply teacher for each half term. I remember asking myself why it was that nobody wanted to stay at our school, but looking around me it wasn't that difficult to see why. Our school building was old and crumbling, we were oversubscribed, and classes were packed. And the first thing anyone ever thought about when they heard our school mentioned was the stabbing that had taken place outside the schools gates in 1999. Perhaps the reason I was so desperate for a teacher to stay was so that I had a better chance of getting the grades I needed to escape one day myself.

Despite the difficulties and challenges of my inner-city school, I still had so much that many young people in similar situations today may not have. My family had a strong work ethic which gave me high aspirations. My teachers worked extra hours to ensure I was truly involved in all my subjects and so that I would be able to get the best grades possible. They instilled a belief in me that if I worked hard, and wanted to, I could walk into any university or any career that I chose, regardless of my ethnic background or social class. When I did finally graduate, I knew I wanted to instil that same belief in others.

My own experiences of school made me decide to become a trainee teacher in a low-income community. The role I now have – leading and inspiring young people, helping them build their futures – is not without its difficulties. I have already come across many tough challenges on my Teach First journey; struggles in managing the workload; constantly marking and planning; dealing with poor behaviour; and overcoming apathy.

Sharing this first challenging year in teaching in a BBC3 documentary may seem like a crazy idea to many. And looking back on what I myself experienced in education, it is easy to think that someone like me would be instantly put off a role in teaching. It was exactly for this reason, however, that I chose to be involved in the documentary 'Tough Young Teachers'. I firmly believe that teaching is one of the most rewarding and gratifying careers, and I saw in this documentary the opportunity to bring to light the many challenges students from more disadvantaged backgrounds can face. I felt it was a chance to express my belief that, with dedicated teachers, and a desire to learn, any student can achieve their potential – and be surprised by the results.

'We need to talk about education' examines this belief, and should go some way to ensuring everyone understands the importance of hearing directly from young people about the reality of growing up in low-income communities, as well as the incredible work being done by those around them to help them build their futures.

The sad fact is that educational inequality is still a reality in the United Kingdom today; How much your parents earn still determines how you will do at school and in life. Yet awareness of the issues around this, and all the factors that can help get a child on the right path, is still fundamentally lacking. It is only by listening, first hand, to the stories of young people, such as those in this book, that we can hope to understand and go on to address this inequality, ensuring every child has the chance to succeed in life.

Meryl Noronha, Teach First English Teacher 2012 Cohort

Introduction

When writing about education there is always a risk that the stories which make up the lives and experiences of pupils get lost, either because they are overwhelmed by technical jargon and statistics or because there is little room for individual narratives in the depiction of schooling systems. Real-life issues – the lifeblood and purpose of education – can be forced to take second place.

It was this human narrative, the reality behind the figures and graphs, that we set out to document when we took on this project at Teach First's request. Teach First is dedicated to combating the odds stacked against certain children, particularly those from underprivileged communities and income groups. But the charity was not after another report or new recommendations. Instead, the challenge they set us was to capture in words and images the emblematic hopes and challenges of today's schoolchildren, parents and teachers. Our approach was to use interviews and workshops to delve behind the scenes into everyday experiences. We wanted to give young people their own voice and allow them to describe the intricacies of life in and around our schools, exploring the role of teachers and the reasons why some pupils achieve their full potential, and others do not.

At the centre of the process was the desire to grasp the realities of educational inequality, to explore its repercussions and follow its ramifications. Educational disadvantage is rarely one thing: it is a chain of issues hooked together. To do justice to its complexity, and the lives of those that experience it day in, day out, we had to trace educational challenges back, not just to the classroom, but to the way they manifest themselves on the street, in the family, in the home, behind closed doors. And this required talking to a wide range of people in different geographical settings across the country, making connections that were not immediately obvious, casting a light on problems that were sometimes only hinted at, asking awkward questions at awkward moments, uncovering uncomfortable truths.

This is the result: a collection of diverse opinions and viewpoints, expressed by those who live and breathe education from within. It should inform and fuel the debate surrounding educational inequality. The book is, necessarily, a rallying call. It is obvious that without renewed mobilisation of civil society, businesses, government and many more, the inequalities in our schooling system will continue to fester. We all need to keep talking about education, taking up the conversation about equal chances and opportunities – just like the schoolchildren, parents and teachers in this book, each offering a chance for change, a possible answer and a new resolve.

Ben Faccini and Greg Villalobos

Chapter 1

What do you want to be?

Ask a student about his or her first day at school and many will recall the disinfectant smell of corridors, the unfamiliar feel of a uniform against the skin, the rush and bustle of schoolchildren in the playground and the name of a new teacher.

Many adults, too, might still remember their first day, waiting for their first lesson to start. Many might also remember being asked, at some point in their school years, what they wanted to be when they were older or where they were heading once all the lessons were over.

It is with one question, 'What do you want to be?' that we decided to start our interviews and writing workshops. The question is far from innocuous. We asked it because we wanted those being interviewed to try to visualise their future and identify or label their aspirations and hopes. When researching the everyday realities of education, this is a powerful opening gambit. It immediately launches a journey into the lives of schoolchildren.

In fact, the question turned into the philosophical basis of this project. The issue of aspiration became the foundation for a whole range of subjects. If an aspiration is to be achievable it has necessarily to bring with it an awareness of potential obstacles. This awareness, in turn, opens up connected issues such as housing, family environment, mind-sets, values, opportunities, friendships, teaching, classroom behaviour, expectations and much more. In this way the hope-filled question of 'What do you want to be?' can paint a detailed picture of a student's relationship with education and the world.

Several students we interviewed did not have a specific future in mind, nothing that could be identified as a recurring aspiration. Many more voiced a clear and enthusiastic aspiration. But in numerous cases that aspiration seemed an elusive dream, as no clear route or next step towards making it a reality was immediately obvious. The dream seemed to fade under the scrutiny of our discussions, as if destined to remain a distant point on the horizon. We were left with the impression that it is not enough to have aspirations – many more pupils had ambitious dreams than didn't. What was often missing was a means of connecting that aspiration to reality, creating actual steps to make it happen. A lot needs to happen in terms of family support, school back-up, advice and use of opportunities for an ambition to prosper. It is into this gap between hope and reality that many schoolchildren fall. Those from deprived backgrounds, in particular, as one teacher pointed out, 'do not know how the system works'. Many had the benefit of families who could make their goal a reality. Others had never been asked questions about the future.

It was striking that young pupils in underprivileged areas often voiced hopes that were in stark contrast to their background. They wanted to be doctors, lawyers, music moguls, entertainment executives and the like. Older pupils in the same areas, however, tended to entertain visions that were more in keeping with their environment. It was as though aspirations got gradually worn down if they were not fed by hope, like clothes that eventually became threadbare. There were also pupils who were already resigned to living in the shadow of the adult disillusionment they witnessed around them. For example, one boy, named Luis, noted with grim acceptance that his future self wouldn't be any different from how he was now. In his picture of his own future, he would still be sitting around, battling with life as he had done with school, thinking about how it had all gone wrong and how he had never got his act together. 'What do you want to be?' can lead to disturbing answers.

We visited schools across England, but with a focus on London, the Midlands and the North East. A fair proportion of the teachers interviewed were trained by Teach First, many were not. People outside schools – notably parents and community members – were also interviewed in each selected geographical area. Their connections to schools varied in a whole host of ways. Slowly a structure for the project began to emerge, driven by the four main questions we were repeatedly asking. It became clear to us that the book, as an open platform for opinions and viewpoints, was best served by being structured by these four specific questions – questions that could be asked of the reader as well. These were: 'What do you want to be?', 'What are you going to do about it?', 'What could stop you?' and 'How can teachers make a difference?'.

Jack
London

'I want to be a sports journalist and I'm passionate about it. I'm good at writing. I like politics too. When I hear politicians I always think I have something to say back. I think work experience is key. The reality of working is important. You need to build up a reputation in a subject. I go on Facebook and Twitter about sporting events and leave comments and people tell me I should give it a go. I think work experience would help make me well-mannered and give me an introduction to the world. I like watching the Olympics, but watching football is the best. I'd like to work for the *Guardian* or *Telegraph* or a magazine called *Sport* for commuters, something more academic, not *The Sun*.'

Rachida
London

'When I first came to this school I would walk through Notting Hill and see the houses and think it was like a dream to have houses like that, but now it's normal for me to see it. I live on an estate. I think to live in one of those houses I have to go to university, but there are so many people right now going to university and they don't even have a job because of the competition. I don't think that dream of that big house is really possible at the moment. Going abroad is good as I speak fluent Arabic and that might give me the opportunity in an Arab country, get a job over there. We come from mixed backgrounds in this school and I know about the world and I think it's good that the school is mixed. I walk and talk with whoever is going to my bus stop and there's a lot of people and we walk down Sheffield Terrace and I pass through the rich places of Notting Hill Gate and I get to Ladbroke Grove. Victoria Beckham lived there for a couple of months and my house is near there.'

Greta
Cleveland

'There's a bit of a stereotype that people just get stuck with. It comes with the area here really, like the north.

'In a way it's just kind of presumed that you're going to work at the steelworks or the fishing industry. Some people think that's the only thing they can do. But I know a lot of people who are aiming higher and want to do something else, something a bit different. My friend, she wants to open an arts centre. But she'd like to work with kids and stuff. And I mean, she's thinking big, like a business plan and having a chain of arts centres. And she's really into the idea and the strange thing is I know she can do it. It's not just one of those, "oh yeah that would be fun but probably never going to do it" type thing, if she really wants it she's going to put her mind to it. She's really conscientious about everything she does. If it's about helping other people she's never going to back out on them, ever. She's always there to listen. She's always a bit hands on about everything. I've never seen her be late to anything! She inspires me, spending time with her, because I know I can be a bit like, "oh yeah, do it some other time," I can be a bit laid back, a bit too laid back to be honest. But spending time with her really inspires me to actually keep going for myself and actually do what I want to do.'

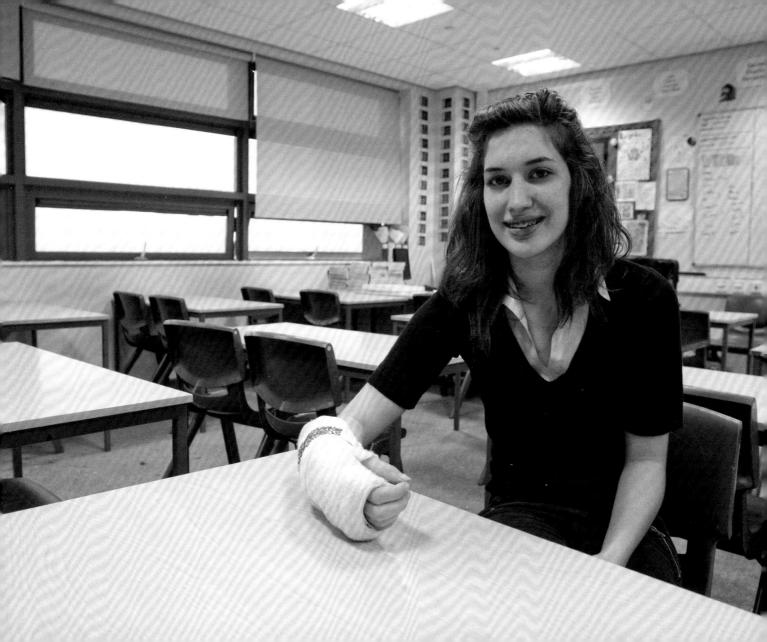

Emily
Barnsley

'I want to live not far from round here when I'm older. I want to work in a nursery, to look after children. Not like a teacher, but someone who looks after them and helps them like when they are at nursery every day. I wouldn't want to be still living with my Mum or asking them for money or drinking a lot or doing something I don't think is going to make me get to where I want to be. I'd like to get to where I want to be before I think of anything like that, like children or getting married or stuff like that. I don't want to be just working in a shop or at supermarket or something like that. I want to get out of school and I can't wait till I can leave and just go to college and start to learn how to do something I want to do when I get older.

'My Dad works away sometimes. He sells security cameras and systems. My Mum works at a shop part-time and my sister goes to primary school. My Mum always said she wanted to be an archaeologist, but she never actually got to be one because she said that she couldn't make a living out it. I don't think my Dad wanted to be what he is now because he doesn't really like his job. They'd like me to get a good job, and they'd like me to have my own house and just make a living for myself ... I'd want to provide for myself and support myself without having to rely on my Mum and Dad all the time. I don't want to be living with my Mum and Dad all my life I want to get my own house and get married and have kids when I'm older and get a nice job.'

Saad
London

'I plan to be the first one of my family to go to uni, and I want it to be a good uni. Then I want to get a good job. That's the basic, and in between I'm going to be happy.

'My family has always pushed me to do the best I can. My friends too. We're not from a great area, but everyone wants to achieve. My teachers are also supportive if you explain things to them. My History teacher has really helped me and made me see what I can achieve. The kind of barriers I've noticed for pupils are small things like not being able to afford a school trip. My Chemistry teacher at GCSE was like a brother to me and that created a relationship and he would engage you and talk to you and I loved Chemistry as a result. My History teacher, too, now makes you feel part of the subject. He makes you feel the passion and why he loves his subject. It's contagious.'

Josh
Cleveland

'My parents go to work early. My sister moved out two years ago. She's twenty. She has a daughter who's just about to be three. I'm an uncle, that's good, apart from the babysitting. My Mum is a support worker. My Dad works in electrical things. I want to get into that too when I leave here. He gets out of the house at 7.15 in the morning. He likes his job a lot. I want to learn things from my Dad and he's shown me how good it is in his job.

'He brought home a booklet with a box and it had all sorts of cables and it was interesting and easy. Quite a few people round here work off-shore, like in Scotland. Two weeks on and two weeks off. I'd like to do it, but you have to be twenty-one. I'd like to go to college for a year and then go straight on site with my Dad, you know, get a trade.'

Leah
Yorkshire

'To other people this area looks quite rundown and the like, but it's not like that. I think I can achieve what I want to achieve here.

'Unemployment is high and there is graffiti and stuff like that. People of our age here are looked upon as disruptive and like kids who hang around on street corners. It depends on how they are brought up, what they want to achieve and their attitude to life, I suppose.

'You have to work at achieving. Some people think you can just glide along instead of improving. I want a future. I don't know what drives me really, but it may be my family and the way they are. My aunt lives with my cousins and I like it where they are and if I have a job and an income that's the future I might also want so I can provide for everyone. I don't know what I want to be when I'm older. I just want education to be able to have the options. I'll probably go on to college and might go on to university. It depends.

'I always want to know why for things. I question things, like in Maths, and I want to know, I question the world, how it works. For me, it's about opportunities and the ones you have to take. I suppose if you don't have those opportunities, you are not going to have the drive to push you on. Opportunities are not given to you. You have to work for them and show you want them. My fear would be if I did rubbish in one of my exams, something like that. I don't want my area or my community to get in my way. My background won't hold me back, I hope. I believe that if you want to work in London you can.'

I want to be: A marine bioligist   because...

- I will be able to travel all around the world
- Discover new species
- And spend time with animals which I love

I refuse to be: A *jellyfish collector*   because...

Workshop 1:
What do you want to be ...?
And what do you refuse to be?

Writing workshops with pupils were a way to harvest first-hand accounts and get to the heart of the issues surrounding schools and education. The objective was to get every young writer to dig deep into their experiences, asking pupils to give details where possible, highlighting specific and tangible moments which would allow us to understand their vision of life and the help or the stumbling blocks they had encountered throughout their school years.

When faced with reticence and apprehension, we sometimes started workshops with simple prompt exercises, asking students to finish off sentences such as: 'I believe ...', 'I fear ...', 'I trust ...', 'I refuse to be ...', 'Life is ...', 'School is ...', 'Family is ...', 'Friends are ...'. Some pupils would fill pages with energetic writing. Others would put down concise, measured sentences, each word carefully thought out. Occasionally, we would read over pupils' shoulders and suggest a new line of investigation or offer a new question. We regularly left schools weighed down by stacks of A4 paper scrawled with lines and lines of spidery handwriting.

I WANT TO BE ...

... inspiring, so I can help people, so people look up to me.

... a better influence for my friends.

...a rich actress.

I want a massive villa. I love acting. I want to rub it in the faces of the people that said I could never do it.

... in a creative profession because I never want to do office work.

... a dentist because it pays well and my aim in life is to make all of Britain have nice teeth.

... me. I want to be who I am, not pretend I'm someone I'm not. I want people to know who I am and why. I want people to respect and appreciate that fact.

...an architect because it's ever changing, creative and free.

...a professional skateboarder because I love it and its my hobby

...a journalist because what you think about influences what others think.

... a happy person. I want to be part of a big happy family.

I REFUSE TO BE ...

... **a cleaner** or work for low payment. I hate not being recognised. I would hate to do lots of work for low payment, and work for a company. I don't like cleaning and stuff.

... **a hobo.** I want to be taster for Cadbury's.

... **a worker in MacDonald's.** People just want food and they aren't polite. It stinks and there is bad pay.

... **unemployed.** I will always work my hardest in education to make sure I never end up unemployed.

... **a bin lady.** The reason for this: you would smell every day, you would get low pay, and you would have to ride around in a big, smelly truck.

... **a criminal** because I don't want to go to jail because of the bad people, the conditions and depression.

...**working in retail** or a cashier because routine is OK, but not on such a scale, and I'm not easily entertained.

... sad, because I wouldn't be content, I wouldn't be happy and I would not have a good life.

... **a doctor** because it takes all your life to do a course for it. When I get good results I'll have more chances. My family will tell me what will be good and bad, and they'll let me think and try before I choose anything.

... **a taxi driver** because you don't get paid enough and you have to drive random people.

Chapter 2

'It can be a good neighbourhood': Byker

Kyle

'I think it doesn't matter where you're from. You've got to achieve what you've got to achieve. If you're from somewhere that's more posh you can probably still do rubbish in school. But then if you're from somewhere that's less developed like Byker, people actually can do good.

'It's your decisions, it's what you've got to do in life. It's up to you what you want to do in school. It's not the community or your family. It's you – you've got to make the decisions about what to do in life. Anyone can do good. It's just what you want to do.'

Leanne

'I was born in the Royal Victoria Infirmary. I lived in Walker for a year, but then I like moved up here and I've lived here since I was two or something. I live with my Mam, Dad, two sisters and a little brother. There never used to be groups for young people here. There never ever used to be young mothers groups either. Now there are. And they've just been getting more people involved. It can be a good neighbourhood. Everyone's friendly. Well half the people are! Everyone knows each other. And everyone's good with each other. We can get called tramps and that, because of where we live. Because of the way it's kept, the way it looks. Rubbish all over the floors. People think because you're from Byker you're little tramps, you're going around pinching stuff and all that. Sometimes you get people who think "oh look at her". I know that shit. They're cheeky and I'm cheeky back. They try and tell me to shut up, especially in holidays, because everyone plays out till late. At nighttime we're like everyone round the estate being noisy and they tell you to shut up because they haven't anything to do. Someone says "ah you're a bunch of bairns, get away, it's past your bedtime" and that.

'People say it's good when you leave school, but it's really boring because there's nothing to do. I would rather be at school, running around like a lunatic and being cheeky. I've been excluded twice. There are community centres. They have dance teachers. I want to be a tour dancer first. What I need is good qualifications and hopefully I'll get there. But I don't think I'll get it in Maths because I've never done well in my Maths exam. I've done one exam and that's it. Some friends sit and smoke buckets in back alleys. Two of them go to college and the rest of them just sit and get stoned all the time. I couldn't really care about them. Just as long as I know I get my future job. They haven't made enough effort in school anyway so ...'

Stephie

'My Dad lived up here for years. I lived with my Mam. Now I live with my Dad. It's all right sometimes. Been here just over a year. Where I used to live was really, really bad. People got stabbed and everything all the time. You get more welcome here in Byker.

'I've got a little sister and a little brother, but I've got two older sisters and an older brother too. I'm looking for absolutely anything [job]. I went to college for two years doing sport. But then in the second year I quit half way through because it was just so boring. And I couldn't be bothered to do all the work.

'I'm on the dole. I do sit around all day, but I don't smoke buckets. I don't take drugs. I smoke, but that's about it. I hardly ever drink. I search for jobs to get out the house. I'm looking for anything because I've got no GCSEs or nothing. Cleaner. Supermarket. Anything. I've been looking for a year and a half. I worked at a supermarket for a couple of months last year, but that was only as a Christmas temp. So that finished after Christmas. And I haven't found anything since. I apply for

things, but I never hear back. It's because I've got no GCSEs or anything. I would just stick with it and do it now, but most colleges wouldn't take me because they look at your records and see that I've quit – they'll not take me back. I just sit on the dole. I get £53 per week. I pay £40 a fortnight rent. I can't move out. Not on the money I'm on at the job centre, no. I get half of my rent paid off by the job centre though. I'm never going to be able to move out. I'll just stop for the rest of my life. It makes me feel horrible. I'd rather be making money and going on holidays, buy a car. I want a big Range Rover. I want a big baby pink one. Have you seen them? I want a job to sort my life out. I'm going to marry a footballer. I hated school. I cannot pay attention for nothing. I've got to be talking and I was always getting things wrong and I was always getting kicked out of school. I would make my kids stay in school. I wouldn't be like my Mam because my Mam let me off with everything. I actually would make my kids stay in school. If I didn't want to go to school in the morning I wouldn't go. School is important because you get an education. You need one. Or else you end up like me! Sitting at the job centre.

'I wouldn't go to London. There's no one friendly at all in London. They just proper troop past you. There's like 500 people walking down the same street. It's horrible. It's all right if you're with someone. I was scared to go on the Tube and everything. People in other areas have good educations because they've been in private schools. We've got to go to community schools. We don't get the chances in life that half the people do. Some schools are better than others. Different schools have different ways of dealing with stuff. Like the schools over here are much better than the school I went to. My school was terrible. It was falling apart. The schools here, they've actually been done up. The teachers actually care.'

Roberta, Youth Worker

'We hand out big boxes of strawberries, blueberries, even exotic fruit, at the youth centre. The normal household, or people round here, wouldn't buy it, or be able to buy big tubs of raspberries because they're £2.99, and the kids here take them home for their parents. I don't think people would be surprised by this, even in posher areas. Everyone knows the climate out there, the work, the jobs, and benefits and everything being cut. And everything is going up, but the money is going down.

'On Wednesday we have "Fair Share" too and we go to the supermarket and get stuff like bread, meat, coffee, tins, stuff that's going out of date. People come in and we make a bag for them. Some of the kids coming in here live on junk food. We have kids coming in here after school, and I'm not exaggerating, you can ask any of the staff, they come in here and go straight to the cupboard. It's because they might have had a cup of tea and a piece of toast for breakfast and a school meal, and when they get home they get a bag of crisps or a sandwich. There are not that many that will sit down at a table.'

Stacy

'I'll push my kids to work. I just hope they do well at school. I'm not the type of person who is going to push them to say "you're going to university and that", I just want them to do whatever they want to do and if I push them they may not want to do it. As long as they try their best at school and they can decide what they want to do. I'm not really pushy.

'I want them to be happy in themselves. I want them to be able to go to school and leave and be able to go to college, choosing what they want to do, so that by 21 or 22 they can have their own house, their car, be able to stand on their own two feet. There are bigger and better jobs out there, whereas in our area there's not much opportunity.'

Alan

'I don't want my kids to follow me in my career. It's too hard my job (industrial cleaning). It's really hard. I want them to be independent, not do what their parents did. I would like them to get a bit of worldly nous about them. The world doesn't revolve around this postcode and this area. They could go away, but it would hard for us to let them go, but if that's what it will take for them to grow up … My job is all about the money. I was brought up by my father and I learned more from him in the first three months after leaving school than I did in the years I was in school. That was just passing time for me. I went to work and I never looked back.

'My kids are my motivation. My kids' future is for them to be able to hit their goals. I can't expect any more from them. It's all about who you've got behind you to help you.'

Annette

'I probably shouldn't say this, but I can see a lot of myself in my son, Kyle. Because I messed about at school. I was the clown of the class. I was easily distracted. I know I enjoyed school because the disadvantaged area I lived in, school took you away from it. But I kind of more saw it as fun rather than learning. I wasn't that academic, I wasn't thick, but I wasn't that academic at school. When I was growing up I used to think that "I cant wait to leave school and leave home."

'I knew you had to be academic to be a social worker. To do anything good you had to be quite clever. And I didn't see myself as quite clever at all. I'm a lot wiser than I thought I was. When I was 15 I was seen as one of the naughty lasses at school. I don't think school failed me, I think I failed myself in education. I think if I had stuck at it, maybe I would have changed the direction. But when I left school and I had done the YTS (Youth Training Scheme), you know, all I wanted then was a baby. Do you know what I mean. Because I think I knew I would be able to do something good. And I knew I would be a good mother. So I knew I might not have been that social worker, but I knew I would be a good mother.

'I don't think it's directly the schools' responsibility. I think the schools can only do what they can do and deliver what they can. It's down to the students and what they want out of it. Because education can be boring. So I think it's down to the determination of the parents to follow it through. The most important years are junior years. You know, to get your kids focused. Because once they're seniors they do change. Their direction changes. Their friends change. And that's the time when they will mess about. And I think if parents sit back and don't encourage and push then they'll have lost it. Not one day have my kids been off school even when they're sick. "I'm not feeling well" – tough you're going to school. And if the school thinks you're not well they'll send you home. That's my motto!

'I'm proud of Kyle's excellent attendance record. There's a lot that he can improve on personally, do you know what I mean, he's got a lot more to offer that he doesn't push himself enough on. And so I tend to keep on top of him for that. He could do more work than he's actually doing right now. And he knows that this is the most important year of his life, and next year, for his GCSEs coming up now. But, at the end of the day, I said it to Kyle and I said it to my other two older sons, all you can do is your best.'

Dear future me,

In 3 years time I will be in college, working
to apply for a photography and hopefully
I will get through. My course will last for
2 years at the end of the course I will
get my results saying that I have past.
At this moment in time I'll be 19 years
old. After my time at college I'll go
up for a house during this time and s
and find a part time job and s
during my driving test and
when I'm 24 I w
BM

Workshop II:
Dear future me …
Imagine yourself aged 30 …

One particularly revelatory writing exercise was to ask pupils to imagine themselves aged 30. What would they be wearing? What might they be thinking? Where would they be living and with whom? Where would they be in twenty or fifteen years' time?

There were huge variations in answers. One student wrote a thank you note, congratulating herself for having hung on and succeeded in her exams, overcoming the trials and tribulations of her twenties. A boy of twelve wrote of fear of family pressures to conform to a future he didn't want – and behind it the fear of the unknown was almost palpable, accompanied by a clear-sighted anticipation of difficulties ahead. When asked to list the main reason their future life plan would work, it was note worthy that most students wrote down 'school'. There were, though, significant numbers of young people who, rather than school, cited family ties, connections and just plain good luck as the best chance to have a decent life.

Dear future me ...
Imagine yourself aged 30 ...

Dear future me

(aged 30), I am writing to you to tell you my life plan and how I am going to achieve it through school. When I'm your age I want to be a pharmacist. How do I achieve this? By revising and learning about medicine and so on. My family helps me by motivating me and showing me what life could be like for me if I become a pharmacist.

Dear me in the future,

I still live with my parents and I've got no job, I'm sharing a room with my brother. This is because I mucked around in lessons when I was a kid and not doing my homework. If I haven't done this then I'm a pilot...

Dear future me,

I would like to start by saying that in many years from now, I want to be a successful person not just in the world of work, but a well rounded human being who gives importance to values and has morals in life. I am yet to discover my passion and which direction I want to head towards in life, whether it is choosing a career in medicine, ranging all the way to a career in the creative industry. What's really important is that I want to obtain contentment in whatever I do. Right now, having the perspective of an 18-year-old in sixth form, the encouraging factors for making the right decision for the future are solely your teachers and your parents.

By the time I'm 30

I would like to be a successful engineer, as well as having other streams of income in my life. This is because I've read that most millionaires have six or more forms of income. School will help me to accomplish what I want to be, because in school I learn about all the jobs out in the world and, in my opinion, knowledge is the key to success and the only way to get knowledge is through school - and it's knowledge that helps a person be successful.

Dear future me aged 30,

I wish an ambitious dream. I wish to have a successful life, to fulfill my education and get a job as a vet. I also hope to have a wife and kids at that age - and I hope that her and my family get along well.

Chapter 3

What are you going to do about it?

Underpinning this project was the belief that each of us has ideas and evidence that could contribute towards a constructive dialogue on how our schooling system might become more responsive to the long-term needs and life chances of the most disadvantaged. We knew that students who had truly suffered from exclusion, from feelings of marginalisation and relegation, would provide the extra insight necessary to that dialogue. We weren't always after grandiose theories and deep philosophies of change. Many of those interviewed offered simple solutions to their own daily dilemmas or described how they had managed to turn things round for themselves. This, in itself, was highly informative of the wider picture.

Some pupils and parents believed quite fervently that it was ultimately up to the individual to create change; that you could still make great things of your life if you had been brought up in challenging circumstances. Teachers supported this – and often singled out children who were succeeding in school despite their background – but they also noted the fragility of these successes. Small setbacks or a family crisis, an episode of bullying, a parent losing a job, moving home and the like could quickly derail a positive trajectory. There was also the risk that a pupil from a low-income family who had been well supported by staff in school would discover different realities when looking for work or training opportunities. It was essential to believe, they said, that a child could pull through despite the odds – and many did – but the basic facts on the ground were that many bright students from disadvantaged backgrounds still did not reach their full potential.

Jahadeel
London

'My dream is to be successful. I'm not entirely sure in what. Perhaps I want to go into medicine, sometimes I feel like being an engineer. There's just so many branches in engineering, medicine is obviously so tough to get into. It's just a really competitive market. I suppose the dream once again is to be successful, I'd like to go into medicine a lot. I think one thing that I might end up struggling with, something I'm quite concerned about is actually myself. I want to do medicine and I want to go on to do all these bright really successful things, at the back of my mind I'm also thinking about all those other people who want to do these bright successful things. And you know, it's not going to be easy. It's quite difficult to describe how supportive my teachers have been. Difficult to label, so supportive, so reliable. Even when it was me being lazy they would put that extra effort in. It's been a really great help.'

Ellie
London

'I don't really know. I want to be rich because then I can provide for my family and buy a car. I have to get a job first. I can imagine working with children or old people. I could do health and social care and childcare. My nan is a teacher and she helps me. She doesn't really motivate me, but if I have a problem she can help me. I would go to a teacher if I have a problem. That's the easiest option. I worry about my GCSEs and I want to get them, but I'm not focused. I'm going to push myself and revise a lot because that relates to the future. I don't want to be poor. That's the bottom line.'

Peter
Birmingham

'My Dad tells me I have to get good marks and if I do he gives me more pocket money. I used to be rude to teachers and answer back to them. I was disruptive. My teacher used to talk to me and explain that I had to change. He spoke to me one-to-one. My Dad tells me not to get into trouble. I've never talked to him about his schooling. I'd like to join the army because I like that kind of working hard and wearing myself out. My brother who's living at my Mum's he was in army. He took me one Saturday and showed me the stuff you do. I have never been to a different country. Sometimes on holiday you end up getting bored and you want to go back to school and then when you go back to school it starts getting boring back there too. In the holidays my Dad goes to work and we have to stay at home and do the chores like wash up, take the dogs out, do all the housework. My Dad does the cooking though. My Mum lives somewhere else. I see her on Tuesdays and Thursdays. I'm not allowed to see my Mum at her house. I have to have a special contact.

'I would like to go to Spain. My cousin went there and she said there was a computer shop and I spoke to her on webcam and it looked really nice and she said it was really hot and you can go out on those paddling boats. I want to go one day.'

Chris, Teacher
Birmingham

'I have encountered educational disadvantage in several ways.
There are the recent immigrant children who can't express
themselves in English – and this must be painful as some are
very bright, as well as the social aspect too of having to cross
borders, their parents seeking employment and a better life,
while their young minds are being formed. The culture shock
is massive. Then there are the British-born who perhaps
sometimes don't have the cultural or economic capital.
Sometimes you catch the eye of a pupil in a certain moment
and you realise what is going on in their heads about their
lives. You understand the potential buzzing around them, but
there is also a feeling of impotence. I only have four hours a
week of contact with each pupil. But I'm often thinking what
is behind the doors when they get home. To apply for the right
school in Birmingham you have to be really on the ball like the
middle-class parents are. What chances are there for those
who don't know the system?'

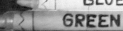

much money

I Want to be a beauty therapist.
Because

- I beline by & looking Good you feel Good.

I refuse to be
I Window cleaner

Workshop III:
Comparing schools

Writing exercises, such as noting down a message for the Minister of Education or drafting a letter to future generations, were methods of getting pupils to value their opinions, to set down their ideas for change on paper. They revealed a strong desire to engage with those they believed to be in charge. There is a certain assumption that school pupils have no political voice, but, given a chance, they readily jumped on subjects such as the rising costs of university fees, budget cuts and unemployment figures. 'What are you going to do?' wasn't just a question for them. They were throwing it back at society. It was as if they were asking: what are you going to change to make our schooling system more inclusive of all and more able to confront the inequalities of society?

Foreign-born students were particularly instructive in revealing the pluses and minuses of the educational system, because they had something real to compare it to. They could see straight away what hadn't worked in their own country – for example, over-strict teachers, or a rigid curriculum. Equally, there were differences that enchanted and surprised them in Britain.

What was your old school like ...?

In my school in Albania it was nice because you don't have to wear a uniform and the lessons were more short and I used to have a lot of friends, but one bad thing was that the teachers slap you if you don't do your homework. And in the school in England it is better because teachers are nice and if you don't do homework they won't hit you, they will just give you a point and I've learned more here because it's easier than Albania.

In my school in my home country of Libya they used to get a stick and whack it on your hand if you were late or absent for a day, but what you can do is let your Mum or Dad write an excuse on a piece of paper and give it to the teacher then the teacher won't hit you. Other than that, the school was very dirty, they never cleaned the floor and never cleaned the windows. The school in the UK is much better because they can't hit you and the schools are always clean.

I miss my home country.

I miss my family. I miss my friends. Schools are different. In England next year I'll finish my secondary school, in Slovakia next year I would be starting secondary school. The level of teaching is really high in Slovakia. The lessons are shorter and after every lesson we have breaks. In Slovakia we have no rudeness in comparison to England. Pupils need to respect teachers and be punctual. There is no form time in Slovakia. The school day starts at 8.00 a.m.

My home country school and the school here are different.

In Somalia if you are late for school the teachers come with the stick and hit our hands and the schools are not clean. Some places and some teachers are sad. The school in England has got a uniform and if you come late you just get detention and this is better and you learn more.

The difference with my school in India and school here is the students' behaviour.

Students mess around in school here, they bully other students and they don't even listen to teachers which is ridiculous. If students do these same things in India there are very strict punishments.

Chapter 4

'I want a future': Cleveland

Shanon

'I didn't think school was important. My Mum knew, but, like, I didn't listen to her. I used to get excluded all the time. Chucking stuff off the balcony. Refusing. Swearing. During a lesson, with a supply teacher, I just got stupid and started ripping stuff off walls. Because other people were doing it and all. And a teacher came in. And, then, I shouted at him. And he took me into his office. I walked out. Just didn't listen. I got excluded for a day I think.

'I went through the stages on behaviour panels. When you're naughty they just review how many "on call's" you've had. It started with the pastoral leader. Then it went to another teacher. Then it went to the deputy. They set targets for you to do within the space of two weeks. And I didn't follow them so it had to move up more. I was the first person in the school to get to the head teacher. That was the last stage. She'd give you targets and if you didn't meet them you'd be permanently excluded or go to a different school for six weeks. The lessons I was struggling with, they'd put another teacher in to help me, or they'd put me in a different room to do my work. Like take me out of the lessons I was struggling with. It was better because I didn't feel that the teachers were helping me much when I was struggling.

'I've calmed down a lot. Caring more. Doing my work. It's changed how I feel about school. It wasn't that easy. It was wrong, and I shouldn't have behaved in school like that. I'm not really sure what I want to do yet (in life), but ... my Mum's brother lives in Australia and they said when I leave school I can go live with them. But I don't know if I want to do that yet. I either want to be a social worker or working with kids. I'm not getting in trouble. Doing bad things. Now I think that I respect teachers a lot for helping me stay in school and that. I'm an inspiration to others. Because, looking back at how I was other times, and like how I am now, I'm a totally different person at school. And the kids say that I inspire them ...

'It's good when teachers listen to what problems you've got. They try to help you. They respect your wishes. Before they moved me to a different English class, if you asked for help the teacher used to shout it out in classroom and tell everyone, which I didn't like because I'm like a shy person. But now, when I'm in my new English class the teacher will come and sit with me and help me. Not like tell everyone.'

Josh, Teacher

'I'm from this area. I've come back here having been away fifteen years and I've really enjoyed coming back, but because I've known those other experiences and opportunities and had the option to go wherever. And I don't think the kids here appreciate that you can go off and do things like I did and not just be focused on this area. You need to open your mind a bit, not that this area is bad, but you need to know you can get away.

'The school I started working with in Stockton was on an estate and there was a shop too. There was no reason to leave the estate for the kids. The school was a real community school. A haven for those kids who had T.V.s in their houses, but had mattresses on the floor and the school was warm and welcoming and friendly. Certain kids, too, of course, didn't want to be at home. Some kids here are in poverty, but it's not as obvious as in Stockton. The problem here is that you can get three generations of unemployed, so the aspirations are non-existent for some of the kids.

'There is no role model for some in the household, no-one who goes out in the morning to work and who comes back in the evening.

'Their role model can be the person who goes to the job centre to get their benefits as that's the way to get money, or the person applying for benefits, or the teenager girl getting pregnant. That is changing. We've only got one pregnant girl here now, but it has been higher in previous years. The three generations of unemployment is a big issue and lots of kids come from farming backgrounds and, again, lack aspiration. They could be more involved in farm management if they wanted, but they work as labourers. They don't see another route.'

Gordon, Teacher

'I feel that I am achieving the goal of having left the pharmaceutical industry. There have been fairly dark days in teaching but the dark days are extremely rare. And in those days I thought I wish I were back in industry working shifts.

'The maxim I gave my friends when I said I was leaving to start teaching, because there was much pointing and laughing, and the maxim I give to trainee teachers, because I've been a mentor for lots of different trainee teachers is "There's not many jobs where you can make a difference every single day." And you can: every day. A daft throwaway line to a vulnerable child can destroy them. And they will stay destroyed for years and years. You can probably remember a teacher you hated because they said one thing to you once. It was like a lance to the heart. The flip side is true in that if you say something positive to a young person or if you make their life more enjoyable, or you give them something or you impart some knowledge that allows them to be more successful.

'It's the rarest and best job in the world, and I do sound like an evangelist but I think that, and I think that because I did something else and I didn't fall into teaching for the want of something else to do. I made a conscious decision "Right I've done that job and I would like to try this job," and it's brilliant and it's rewarding.'

Amy

'For me a teacher has to be strict, like, to get it through to people. And I think that if you respect a teacher they respect you back. But if you don't respect them, then obviously they are not going to respect you back. I think if you want to be a teacher, if you are a teacher, then you'll want the kids to learn. Sometimes you learn something yourself that day. Every teacher has a different way of teaching. Some have practical ways, like science. I do enjoy science and I've really improved in science. All teachers are different,. They all have their different ways of teaching. Respect is really important to me. I respect Mr D. I do, because I've improved in Maths. I went up to a higher level. Sometimes I don't respect teachers because other people don't respect the teachers and I feel that I have to like, go with their lead. And if I don't go with them they won't be my mate anymore. Do you get me?

'I got into the wrong crowd in Year 7. But now I've got a nice group of close friends and out-in-the-open friends I like to see around school. And I've got into the right crowd now and I know where I want to go. I want to be a singer, just doing gigs and that. I need to like knuckle down in music. I'm definitely not going to be roaming the streets drinking. I'm not going to be doing antisocial behaviour in lessons like other people in the school do now. I'm going to get a job and I want to have a life, not like a low life, low and roaming the streets like some people do when they're 23, 22.'

Jamie, Teacher

'For some of the kids here teaching good lessons is not enough. You've got to make the kids believe you'll move heaven and earth to help them otherwise they aren't going to make the grade. But how do you do that? Part of it is saying to them "I'm going to be on the phone to your parents so that when you do something good your parents are going to hear about it". I keep saying a positive phone call takes 90 seconds. If I can do three of those per lesson per day then that's about 20 minutes in total and that's the same amount of time I might have to take for a kid mucking around and with the negative phone call to follow up. So if I can get them on side, and when they are good they get that phone call home, it is 50 times easier in lessons.

'I think in the first few weeks I realised that if you just ring up parents for negative things that has quite a limited effect and they say things like "we know" and "he's like that at home as well" and that kind of attitude. If you keep beating someone with a stick then eventually they are to ignore the stick. It has an effect as the kid will say, "Sir, if I do really well in this lesson, will you phone my parents?"

'The best phone call you can have is if you ask to speak to a Mum or Dad and they say "who is it?" and I say "it's Mr Douglas, and I had your child in my class today and I just wanted to say that she/he was absolutely brilliant and enthusiastic and please make sure they know I've called" and the parents are blown away and I've never had a phone call like that, that hasn't ended up well. That's an incentive to do it. That gets paid back in spades by the kids too. All the more when you do it for kids who have little else in their lives, when you do something for them, off your back, in your own time, it means everything to them.'

Alex

'At school a few people kept calling me names. And I didn't really get a good education before because of them always taking the mick. And I used to sit quite a few seats down from them so they'd start throwing cans and stuff at me so I'd throw them back. And then there was another lad, I can't remember his name, he used to get bullied by them. He used to argue and start fights, but I didn't want to start a fight because it was a waste of time me starting a fight and losing an education through that. So I just kept on trying to ignore them and it would just keep going on and on. But then, like they started saying "your Mum's this, your Mum's that," blah blah. They started bringing up stuff about my Dad. But I've lost my Dad. I didn't even know him when he died. Eventually, once they found out that, they just didn't want to say nothing else. Then Kate came in and we started having meetings with her. I started getting stronger so I wasn't really that fussed about getting bullied.

'Miss B., she's head of school and that and Miss F. she always helps out with bullying and everything. She's there for me. I used to have a peer mentor. But now I'm actually a peer mentor myself and I mentor a little Year 7. Miss F. and I went and saw Kate first. It was quite hard at first, because I was too scared to talk to her because it was the first time I'd ever seen her. But now like, I go up to her all the time, just bring it all up, everything. She has strategies, stress balls, stuff like that to try and keep my anger down and that. She'd say things like "try to do this next time". Or she has strategies, she'd say three or four and one of them actually usually works. Miss F., too, talks to the bullies and says "this isn't right, don't carry on." Sometimes they don't listen, but eventually if it keeps going on they'll end up getting isolated for a day, or they end up getting excluded for a day and get detentions and all that. And eventually people learn.'

Liam

'The first day I met Mr W., we were all sat at the front. He got introduced. He tried telling me what to do, and, er, I wasn't the best of students at that time. So, basically, I said to him "don't tell me what the f**k to do you're only a supply. Get the f***ing hell out my way." That was when I was 15. And in basically Year 7, Year 8, Year 9, Year 10 I did no science work and I had Year 7, Year 8, Year 9, Year 10 work to catch up on. So I would stay back till 6 o'clock at night. I think one day a week, sometimes two so I could get science finished. And I came out with two Cs in science. I had a lot of support from Mrs T., she was a real success in our lives, she still is a part of our lives. If it hadn't been for her we wouldn't have got through the school the way we did. She calmed us down a lot.

'With the other teacher, like I explained, that first day was awful. You know it's just like some random person going into the class telling you what to do, "I'm not having that!" But then we like started to understand that he cared about all the science work really and he wanted to get us through it as much as he could. You know he didn't give up, there were plenty of kids in here that would take him to the limit every week, and the next week he would still push them and push

them to get the work done. I mean there's not many teachers that will do that. If you treat kids with respect they'll treat you with it as well. It's a saying isn't it, if you give me respect I'll give you respect. I just started to have a laugh with him. I mean some days I was naughty. Some days I was like "I can't be bothered today, I've done all my work this week". And then some days you wouldn't even hear me I'd be down scribbling, sharpening my pencil all the time to get it done.

'I was actually quite surprised. I thought I was only going to get two Cs but I came out with 6 Cs, two Bs, an F, an E and a U. So I mean, for a lad whose got dyslexia, it's come out pretty good because of Mrs T. She's like a hero to all of us.'

Chapter 5
What could hold you back?

Asking pupils what is preventing them from achieving their potential is like opening up floodgates. Some pupils hesitated a few seconds before expressing their aspirations for the future, but most quickly described some of the barriers to success in both school and society. These often sounded like a litany of societal problems. Many, though, were distinctly personal and rooted in difficult relationships with family members or about self-perception.

Just as pupils in London and other cities expressed a greater range of aspirations, so city pupils from schools in challenging circumstances were more explicit in listing the obstacles facing them. The reason, they stated, was because they clearly understood what separated them from what society termed 'success'. They witnessed it on a daily basis, every time they walked past expensive shops in city centres, every time they travelled on buses through better-off neighbourhoods or simply when they observed high-earning professionals going about their lives on the streets. In many ways this comparison to others defined who they were and what they wanted out of life. This wasn't necessarily the case in outer-urban or semi-rural settings, for example in Yorkshire, where students spoke of a lack of examples of success. Isolation there seemed to add another layer to the barriers in front of young people.

'It's not always easy,' one boy said quietly when asked what stood between him and achievement at school. 'Unlike me, not everyone wants to learn in my class.' Certain themes such as this emerged on a regular basis. The subject of friends, friendship groups and other pupils was a recurring motif. Several students spoke of the influence of peers as something that could either hold them back or propel them forward. A dynamic group of hard-working pupils was inspiring. It was difficult to concentrate, however, if other pupils saw school as a chance to mess around or were deliberately apathetic in lessons. It was equally hard to carry on being successful if many in the class had a negative view of achievement, or even of interacting too enthusiastically with a teacher. Attitudes, cliques, classroom atmosphere, pupil self-worth and motivation returned time and time again in discussions, especially in schools that were deemed to be challenging. The extreme version of anti-school mind-set appeared to be adherence to gangs in and around schools as well as other pernicious allegiances. It was not just pupils who suffered in these situations, but teachers too, as they often had to break through entrenched disaffection to get the attention of a class. Quite a few students said they didn't believe in their own capacities, that they weren't cut out for school and that it was 'just the way things go'.

The influence of the family was often the hardest issue for pupils to discuss, maybe out of pride, a justified sense of privacy, or even because of family dynamics. The economic status of the family, the language spoken at home, the cultural norms of parents, attitudes to education and teachers were all potential barriers as well as possible facilitators of success too. It was very instructive in this context to talk to children from immigrant backgrounds. Their contrasting experiences of home life were particularly revelatory of the practices of many British-born families. How was it possible – some British-born children wanted to know – for pupils who had only arrived in Britain a few years previously without a word of English to be already getting top grades? Immigrant children (with cultural backgrounds as diverse as China, Albania, India and South Korea) offered some pertinent clues. Maybe, they said, it was because they were very rarely allowed out after school and because they studied more than their peers? Maybe they had different relationships with teachers? Many foreign-born children specifically spoke of wanting to help their parents in later life, to repay them for all their sacrifices. That was a major source of motivation in school.

Teachers had often spent many an hour in parents' evenings seeing first hand what factors hindered pupils and which ones helped them. Parental engagement with a child's education was not always a prerequisite of achievement, but there was no denying that it created more auspicious conditions for learning. A teacher with an ally at home was undoubtedly more effective.

Teachers and students were both able to give key views of what the barriers were like in the actual classroom. Maths teachers particularly spoke of pupils being intimidated by the subject, not helped in many cases by parents who had also struggled with Maths at school. This, of course, was true of English as a subject too – all the more so in families where English was not the first language. Other classroom issues could also be indicators of wider problems both inside and outside the school: specific learning difficulties and needs, a lack of subject knowledge, bullying, poor relationships with other pupils, non-attendance, disruptiveness, poor concentration, to name but a few. Teachers' measures, particularly when it came to discipline, were sometimes seen as a hindrance by pupils who had a different view of their contribution to the class. A barrier for a pupil could be a frustration for a teacher.

Kimi
London

'When I arrived in London from France a year ago, it was just an enormous sense of relief. I was going to live on my own with my Dad for the first time. Nothing could have prevented my happiness that first day in London. I felt strong and confident, full of hope. I was booked on the international baccalaureate course at Westminster Academy and I was going to do my tennis.

'Now I know Britain is a closed circle, and if you're not rich or in that circle, you won't get anywhere. It's about connections and hierarchy, full stop. It doesn't matter how good you are, it's who you know. And if you don't know the right people then you're not welcome.

'My Dad managed to find a coach to introduce me to a private tennis club. I went to play and the coach was impressed by my skills. The head of the club saw me from her office and made a fuss about my scruffy trainers. She got the coach to ask me to stop playing and leave the premises. She didn't even dare come and tell me herself. I felt really humiliated. It wasn't just that she thought my shoes were shit, I felt as if my whole life was being called shit too.'

Toby (Parent of Kimi)
London

'My son, Kim, has huge talent, enthusiasm and initiative, but I feel he can lose his way without the clear structure he had in France.

'You can do whatever you want if you really put your mind to it, but it has to come from you. Kimi does have amazing persistence, but, I know, he feels the world around him isn't necessarily with him. I certainly didn't fix a vision for any of my kids. I want them to develop naturally with unconditional love and not feel disappointment and not feel crushed by expectation from me. I say that because my own vision as a child was compromised by what my parents expected of me and how they reacted to my successes and failures. They were very affected by how they were viewed by other people and their opinions. They felt you had to do things even if it wasn't what you wanted.'

Cyrus, Teacher
Barnsley

'I remember there was one lesson when we were doing distances and there was a simple question: what's further Manchester or the Sun? And quite a few of them put Manchester and I just couldn't understand why. They explained, well, to get to Manchester you've got to take like two trains and that takes hours, but the Sun's just there! And that's the logic "oh you can only see what's in front of you". And then the idea that actually if it's further away, if you can't see it, then it's just too far.

'What I've found quite frustrating, especially at a higher end almost is that the kids that are really bright and get good grades, and actually have a good work ethic, don't realise just what they can do with their lives and the possibilities and the potential that they have – they just don't realise, they don't think they're good enough. The amount of under-confidence in so many kids is quite disturbing.'

Sammy
London

'Some people in higher sets at school think you're dumb because you do lower tests. They look down on us. They say stuff. Teachers accompany you to detention and you feel like a kid. They always think you're up to something. It makes me want to prove them wrong. You can get a reputation in school, a bad reputation and it stays with you. School can be fun, but not when you're labelled. I get in trouble for fighting. I had a fight with him (pointing at a boy opposite), but we're friends now. They set us up. We were pushed into it by people. They sent us to a place where people are permanently excluded, where they have behavioural problems and the like, and they treated us like we were mental. Each person had someone following them around. There was another school opposite and they came in and caused trouble. There were people kicking down doors. There were fights. We have fights, but we're friends again. There are people who push you into fights because they are bored.

'My parents are more like friends, but if I get into trouble they will lecture me and tell me their example. They won't tell me off. My Dad can't tell me nothing too much as it would be hypocritical, he got excluded from every school he went to. He got excluded when he was 11. He's like "learn from my mistakes".

'For me the problem is that there are no youth clubs. There are no second chances, if you get a bad label you have to live on benefits and you don't get enough money, only a little bit for clothes and food, but you can't live on it. The rich stay rich. There are no equal chances. I think if you make a mistake at school you should still have a second chance of getting a job like anyone else.'

Casey
Birmingham

'I'm not from here. I moved to Birmingham about a year ago. I live in an area called L. Some of the kids from there come to this school. They are good children. But basically, they see themselves as something different, but if you actually talk to them and get to know them they are actually good people. They like attention. They are disrespectful to teachers to make everyone laugh, but if you're like that you haven't got manners. They say "I don't care about school", that kind of attitude. They are not going to get anywhere in life. In the future they are going to think "I wish I'd paid attention." Those type of people if you don't do what they say, they say that you're like "so and so," you know what I mean? They are jealous if you're better than them at school. I don't care what they think. I just do what I'm doing. I stick to my path. My Mum told me at the beginning what was going to happen at school and what was not going to happen. I did get myself on a wrong path, but I picked myself up.

'She doesn't want me to be like her. She left school early. She's only 27. She thinks she took a bit of a wrong turning at school. They (the L lot) they don't think. They do things straightaway and think after. They comment on everything you do and watch you all the time. If someone keeps calling me a name they will keep at it until I stand up for myself. But they have not stood up for themselves. Their families, their Mums don't know what they are doing. They don't even know where they are. They come back at 10 in the morning and they don't take an interest in their lives. Their friends might manage to pick themselves up but they don't know the difference from wrong or right.'

Josh
Cleveland

'I think my mates are perhaps the ones who might be a barrier. When I'm in Science I'm good even if I'm with my mates, but other times it's always in the back of my mind to mess around. I know people who mess around, but what are they going to get out of school, what are these five years going to be for? Most of my mates' Dads work at Corus (mining company) and they might get their sons in. My Dad only just started in his business, but I hope most of my friends will get jobs and not be on the dole, getting paid for nothing, just sitting around.'

Phil, Teacher
London

'I have come across disadvantage. It jumps out at you from time to time. I was shocked to discover, when I asked the students to bring in calculators, that some of the pupils didn't have one because they couldn't afford it. One child said she couldn't afford a pencil case either. I told them I would write a postcard home to congratulate them on their achievements and one girl told me not to bother as as there was no-one there to read it. She lived in a hostel.

'Beyond this, the main shock for me has been to see how the students change in attitude from Year 7 to Year 10 and 11. They are really motivated at the beginning, at least you can't see the difference between the kids' various backgrounds. Those on free school meals seem to be doing as well as those who are from better-off families. Then, gradually, it's as if the desire for learning falls away for some and it becomes cool to not do well. Of course, I question myself if kids display this pattern or others behave badly. Sometimes I discover it's because they have found some questions too hard or an explanation hasn't worked. I analyse the problem and that's how I motivate those who are struggling or those who are less-advantaged. I have to keep an eye on those who are either too loud or those who are too quiet. It's in those two extremes where the problems lie.'

Seb, Teacher
Birmingham

'There is a gap between student aspirations and how they are going to get there. All their aspirations are quite materially based or professions like doctors, but most don't understand how to get there. They don't understand their situation. Some of their dreams relative to the school are great, but relative to the country they will be lucky if they even do a tiny bit of what they want. If you were to pick a typical student they might well be apathetic at school, but be aspirational in terms of finance. They kind of want their cake and eat it. Of course, many are not like that and many are some of the most inspirational people I have ever met. There are kids who are getting A*s when two thirds of them are not passing Maths or English. Others, it seems, sometimes want the indicators of success, like new trainers, but the rest – the hard work and the education – isn't visible.

'The important thing is perhaps their role models. There are kids on free school meals who have an iphone and the problem is the aspiration to the item rather than a degree certificate. I had one girl who came from Iran aged 12 and she couldn't speak a word of English and now, aged 14, she is top of the top English set, above all her British-born peers. It should be embarrassing almost for the rest of the class, but they don't necessarily seem to care if they're in bottom sets. I think family is key, but there is a level of deprivation before that too, within wider society, which goes even deeper.

'Even students who are seemingly apathetic, I see their families at parents' evening and they are committed, but just don't know how to get there.'

Toby (Parent of Kimi)
London

'I had a strong passion for art and making things from early on, but that was not my background. I was on a collision course with my parents and school and my father had compromised his own vision and he had done what he had to do and not what he wanted to do. I was thrown out of school at 16 and my parents made me do my A-levels but I failed them anyway and I was incredibly disillusioned with school from the age of 7. I just didn't learn in that environment. I never had a teacher who inspired me. I was very negative about life as a result. I felt morbid and felt divided between being happy as a person and what I needed to do to fit into school. That affected me. So I got into building when I left school as it was tangible. I had wanted to go to art school, but I wasn't confident enough and being a builder was like proving I was a real man and I felt more liberated by it. I also wanted to be a tennis player, but I had no structure for that. I felt it was impossible and it saddens me to have to tell my son that now too. I want Kimi to get to the point where he's not at a loose end.'

Social class.

I think Posh people have a better life compared to the people on the streets, because they have an education and they have everything they need in life. but people

Script

How was your day at school?

Yeah it was ok

Workshop IV:
What is social class?

Many pupils, particularly in the writing exercises, raised matters that were harder to pin down and which had their roots deep in the broader inequalities of the country: social class, accents, perceptions of teenagers in society, postcode segregation and what they saw as the nepotistic networks people weave in society to protect their privileges. While some children declared the class system outdated, others said it was alive and kicking.

What is social class?

Social class is upper/middle/lower and how rich you and your family are.
The higher the class, the more successful you are likely to be. There is a big gap between upper and lower classes.

I don't like Oxford and others of these kinds of places, as they have always been privileged and are a prime example of the problems with the class system.

It's determined by wealth. The upper class are treated better. It is a judgement, a label.

In my eyes, social class is equilibrium. No-one is higher up than another. Everyone is equal in their own way. Whether your personality or lack of knowledge is different, you are all still equal in your own way. Everyone should be able to have a conversation or anything with someone without feeling inferior or superior.

I would like to go to Oxford or Cambridge

because they are highly recognised universities and I would achieve high levels of intelligence and the people there would all be working for the same thing I'm working for, but I wouldn't like to go to Oxford or Cambridge too because most people there would come from a rich background and they might look down on me. I probably wouldn't get in because I don't speak in their 'posh' way.

It's like a private school

where you are more likely to benefit in the future.

Class is the amount of income that you receive.

It's job status, hierarchy. Poorer people get less opportunity but will use those they have to full advantage, richer people have many opportunities, but will not use them to full advantage.

Chapter 6

'They're smart ... but they're ruining their future': London

Nadim

'I'm the kind of person who thinks you can choose what you get into or not. I realise that some stuff is wrong, but some people I know are into that stuff. They're smart too, but they're ruining their future and I'm kind of learning from their mistakes.

'A friend of mine, used to be very smart, very clever, and now he's gone down the route of drugs, going out, seeing girls instead of revising – and me I used to be into going out and stuff, not taking drugs, but I changed. I looked at my grades in Year 10 and I had all Ds and it hit me and I realised I had to change. Teachers and family were important in turning me around. It was for my Mum too. I didn't want to disappoint her.'

Jack

'I live in Chelsea, West London, and my bedroom is full of Chelsea Football Club posters. I'm a huge Chelsea fan. It's quite a small room and I share it with my brother. A few shelves for books and a T.V. My brother is 25 and I'm 15. The age gap does cause tension and he wakes me up coming home late or sometimes he gets up early. It affects how I sleep. He is a part-time football coach and he's at university to try and become a sports scientist and he's studying like me. In Chelsea you've got a huge divide, the richest people and loads of estates there too, and people think I'm rich when I tell them I live in Chelsea, but the reality is much different. The conception is completely wrong. We live in a mansion block split up into lots of flats on the road and there's a Sainsbury's too and there's a communal garden that's kept quite nice.

'If you look at this school, generally, not everyone comes from the best background, but if you look at the top band their parents have more chance, their parents have more education and they then have money to buy revision books and a desk and they have more time to tutor and more space in their house.

'When you have a small bedroom and everyone has to work too, it's a lot harder for people who are not as rich as others and rich people can go to private schools. I think in a state school you've got to make the most of your options. People stereotype you if you come from a state school, if you go into a shop with your uniform the security guard will be looking at you even if they don't know your school.'

Nadia

'It hasn't always been obvious. Not at all. I only got my act together two years ago. I started studying and understanding what school was about then. Before that I was a right chav, I was hanging out with the wrong people, I had the bad kind of dreams, the wrong language, and attitude, the wrong life, the wrong clothes. I was trying to be something I wasn't. I was young and I was under the influence of the older ones. People warn you, but you don't hear them. My family educated me on the negatives, but I couldn't see what the wrongs were. There were fake people around me. They were chums, but I couldn't see them really. I sometimes say these days you don't even need to have sex to have your innocence taken away.

'People would cuss my shoes. The society is like that now. You know, I started wearing make-up a few years ago because they were teasing me. I used to be so insecure. Now I wear it all the time. I've got used to it. I don't think they would recognise me if I didn't put it on. Going home I'd be thinking why are they calling me things, cussing me. Everything is about appearance. It was the older boys and others too. When they move on in life they are going to cause trouble, even end up in jail or be drug-dealers. But I have goals now. I want to open a bakery. I say hopefully. I know now what I want to be doing. I am prioritising my education, I'm going to be picking out my opportunities. I know my rights and my wrongs these days. I understand what I need.

'When I look back on this school. I'm going to look back and laugh because it made me a better person. Before I had fake friends. It's helped me analyse what kinds of people there are, I can judge characters, it'll help me at college.'

Steve

'If I go from my house and I go up the hill there are some huge houses and it looks like the people there are enjoying their lives. It's looks like a movie or something. Those people have more opportunities. If they were to apply for a job and they say they went to their school and I say I went to my school then they would probably get the job, because they went to that kind of school. Their school has a reputation for hard work. It has a name. Everyone knows about it and they can get into wherever they want. They have been in private school since nursery and they stay in that till college. Their families help them and they pay and they want the best opportunities for them.'

Danielle

'About half the kids from our school walk home and half get picked up. A lot stay at the end of the road chatting. There are problems around here when gangs come in, it can cause conflict when there are clashes. Everyone can be in the shops down by the station and then there will be gangs from other areas and they see whoever they don't like and there is a big fight and then the police come and some people are idiots and people want to get involved. I'm a girl so I don't feel I'm going to be targeted, but people pull up in cars and everyone runs when the police come. If I hear something is happening I do feel the need to check people are O.K. I'm not a target.

'My family, my Mum knows it happens, especially down by the station. She hates the fact that I might have seen things like that. It's about territory and different areas. Say someone is from one area and someone else is from another, they fight about that. It causes complicated situations. Only this part of Brent is upper-class, but other areas here of London, like East London is full of gangs. This generation feel the need to fight over post codes. There is a connection between what your parents want and what you want out of life. I know the Mums of people in gangs, it's because they have lost control of them.

Most are from troubled backgrounds. Parents moving out, on and off, people switching love, or trying to fit in.'

Ali, Teacher

'There is also a problem, with some kids, that they feel they have to live up to this "bad-ass" reputation. It's not widespread, but some don't want to be seen to be trying. I teach Year 7 through to Year 13 and it gets worse as they get older, before improving again. Initially in Year 8 they do all they can to improve, but by Year 10 they have their peers watching and some don't even want to be seen putting their names on their exam papers. Some kids make negative progress. One kid refused to pick up his pencil and write his name in the exam. I took him aside and I showed him my spreadsheet with everyone's marks and my notes of what I needed to do and where the difficulties were so I knew where to help and it was a bit of a realisation for him. I get the kids to see how much I'm putting in myself. He did his mock this time round.

'I like challenges and that's what hooked me into teaching. I thought I'd love it because of the Maths and I dreaded the mentoring side of things, but it's turned out to be the other way round. The key thing is how to use the knowledge you get from the students and when you plan a lesson incorporate something for them – such as a love of music or something.'

Katie, Teacher

'You can have kids who first say "that's so boring" when I talk to them about Tess of the d'Urbervilles, but then I get to see it through their eyes and it's amazing. I love it. One girl said to me recently, "Miss, I don't know what you've done to me. I go home and I analyse everything and pick everything apart." So for me, English is not so much about them writing the perfect business letter, but about their souls and their minds. Of course, they need to read and write as a skill, and it's a crucial part of their education, but I think it's also vital to have their minds lifted, to be able to critique the world. Literature allows for that and it is also about real-life situations. *Tess of the d'Urbervilles* is about an outcast and her struggles. The subject is real. It matters. We see her choices. It's an invaluable lesson for teenagers, for their life. It brings out all the things they experience.

One girl. I taught her A-level. She was followed by the child protection people. She had a terrible life, but she was heading to Oxford. She was a brilliant student, naturally bright and very able. I would tell her that she was going to be able to walk away from her past life and create a new world for herself. Then, at the last minute, she didn't turn up for her A-level exams. We sent a taxi for her, but, when push came to shove, she couldn't do it. Some don't know how to grab your hand. I can't take the exam for them. At the end of the day, they have to have parents who will fight for them too. There was nothing we could do as teachers, we weren't able to act on that last tiny bit. It broke my heart.

'The teenagers I teach have tough lives. They want to know how others have suffered. Real-life books do that, but so does fiction. Books are like therapy and they want a mirror of themselves. They want authors who understand their lives.

'For me the students need consistency and reliability from a teacher. I hope I deliver consistently good lessons and I say to the pupils that if they listen and absorb things carefully they will succeed and get good grades. I tell them that education is their way out and, I suppose, for many of the kids that don't succeed it is because they don't know how to take that opportunity.'

I want to be ~~a doctor and~~ successful in life.
- ~~so I can save people lives.~~
- ~~keep that people in life~~ I can get a job.
- & so I can earn money

I refuse to be

~~enjoy learning English.~~
My favourite subject is English
I'm good at maths.
I am the best at P.E. & sports

Workshop V:
Where do you do your homework ...?

Housing was stated as a major hold-all barrier for many, with accompanying issues such as cramped conditions at home, sharing a bedroom with siblings or parents, having no room for a desk to do homework, not being able to withdraw anywhere to read or write in peace. The distance of a home from school was generally felt to be a factor of disadvantage, particularly by those who had to travel long journeys, often changing buses several times. Ironically, however, some saw it as a benefit to be a long way from school and the influence of potentially noxious peer groups.

Where do you do your homework ...?

I do my homework on the sofa watching T.V., because I don't have to force myself to do the homework that way and I'm not under pressure. The room is light blue and has good lighting, it is openly spaced, so I don't feel claustrophobic. The table I do it on is hard and wooden, it is flat so it doesn't wobble. I often get distracted by the T.V.

I do my homework on the floor, the floor is golden cold. It hurts me to lay on it. It is hard, but a good writing surface. It enables me to take happy breaks and to fidget. I also slide around to help me focus.

My bedroom is a mess. My bedroom is blue, something is in every corner and I have piles of stuff on my stairs waiting to be taken into my room such as clothes, books, teddies that have never been touched, etc. I do my homework wherever there is an empty space, most of the time it's the sofa, my bed or my desk. There is always music blaring and a box of sweets to keep me company. And I usually have my fat black cat sat on my book to make my homework even more annoying.

I have a desk that is covered in rubbish

(like my empty hamster cage). I do my homework on it, to do this I end up chucking all the things on it on the floor. The room is almost always covered in an off-white light, and my baby brother is crying in the next room so my homework is unbearable to do. My chair is broken and the wheels on the bottom don't roll so I don't have a way of getting comfortable.

I do my homework in the bathtub.

When I get back from school I say hi to my mom and get my water bed, put it in the bathtub and run the water. I pretend that I'm a sailor and I'm at sea. The splashing of the waves calms me after an ecstatic day of school. I concentrate on nothing else but the words in front of me until my brother decides I've been in the bath too long.

My bedroom is shared by my sister,

and we each have a bed in the corner. We each have some drawers for our clothes and share a wardrobe, and we have a shelf full of every kind of toy and other junk. The walls are yellow, decorated with faded swirls. We have no desk or playstation or nintendo, Wii, but don't mind. We have each other (when we're not arguing). I do my homework sitting on my bed, the book propped up on a hard base so my handwriting looks okay.

Homework is in front of the T.V.

because it might give me answers from game-shows, like 'Pointless' for example.

Chapter 7
How can teachers make a difference?

Some students noted with delight that teachers often managed to introduce references to their hobbies, personal preferences and even past conversations into lessons. For them this was proof that a teacher was conscious of their needs and was tailoring lessons to suit them. While only a few teachers recognised such awareness in their pupils, others observed that they regularly explained the effort they were making to their pupils as it was a useful mechanism for demonstrating a common commitment between student and teacher – a chance to make each lesson a real period of learning.

Pupil perceptions of teachers are absolutely critical to understanding how a teacher can make a difference, particularly to a child from a deprived home. When asked to pin down what made a teacher particularly important, many younger pupils almost immediately said, 'if lessons are fun' or 'when you laugh and learn at the same time'. Older pupils spoke of 'mutual respect', and 'good relationships'. Wanting something more specific than this, we pushed pupils of all ages to provide further arguments and details. Some of the beneficial teacher characteristics most cited by pupils were: a skill for talking with students, an understanding of students' lives and worlds, a good sense of humour, an ability to stand up for pupils when problems occurred, a strong connection with parents or families, a solid subject knowledge, a capacity to keep a

class under control and a real talent for inspiring – not to mention an aptitude for not giving out too much homework.

It is hard to think of any profession other than teaching where so many different attributes are required of one person – and this often came up in discussions with teachers as they grappled with how they could make an extra difference to a student's results and life. Sometimes, for instance, teachers were fully aware of the difficulties of underprivileged children, but it was a battle to meet their individual needs above those of others in a class of twenty or more students. It was daunting, many new teachers noted, to have to get used to the enormity of the teaching task (preparing lessons, improvising questions, managing behaviour, enthusing and inspiring on a subject, keeping track of teaching shortcomings, etc.) and be able to address problems in pupils properly.

The issue of teacher quality concerns pupils, teachers, families, schools and education authorities alike – and for good reason. Pupils were pretty unanimous in saying that an inspiring teacher made a patent difference to their lives in school and their academic results. With teachers they liked and appreciated they learned more. With teachers they didn't appreciate as much they tended to be more shy about sharing work or asking questions and, crucially, be less likely to try and prove their academic worth. Teachers were more than aware of these features, but were not going to deny either that family dynamics and a student's home life were also huge factors in school attainment. Often those two worlds of home and school clashed, and it was up to the teacher to manage the spillover into the classroom and to find ways of talking to a pupil about challenges.

Chris, Teacher
London

'One face of educational disadvantage, for me, is the white working-class kids. They don't necessarily feel aware of the true extent of their disadvantage. They don't always see the impact home life has on their schooling. To them it's a form of reality. I have one girl who was taken into care and lived with a foster family before a solution was found. The level of turmoil in her life was such that it wasn't surprising that she didn't know how to behave in class. There needed to be people in school who could almost mother her and take on that parental involvement. I go both for the soft touch as well as the discipline. I would have meetings with her every week and a lot of it was building trust with a view to the future and trying to be able to have more serious conversations with her later on. As head of year, you do take on that kind of pastoral role and you get to know pupils and you can't walk away. I have a boy of 12 and his mother is only 25. She was 13 when she gave birth to him. She really struggles with reading and writing and her son is very weak as a result, and it's been a real struggle to get her to engage with school as she can't read the letters sent home. Now she is in regular touch with the family support person at the school and she comes in once a week and has joint literacy lessons with her son.

'One of the largest problems is lack of awareness of parents of how much power they do have and the impact they could have. Middle-class parents tend to keep teachers on their toes more, but in this area a lot of the parents don't speak English and don't have an educational process themselves. Some parents are quite passive and don't want to challenge their own children. Some won't come to parents' evening because of the language barrier and feel intimidated by school. I had a lad who had just come to the country and his English was shaky, but he was progressing fast and his father came to parents' evening and I launched into praise about how good the boy was and then I stopped because I realised he hadn't understood a word. The father made a thumbs-up and then a thumbs-down gesture, wanting to know which it was. I made a definite thumbs-up and he hugged his son.'

Amber
Barnsley

'I live a mile from school. I've been coming here for a year. This school is more modern, bigger, it's a better place. People act different. In the old school they were running riot. You couldn't get an education. In this school it's calmer. It's stricter. In my old school, people threw stuff and teachers shouted. There was nothing to learn with. It wasn't very nice. Here you come in through the front door and it has space and you can walk without people pushing you. It's a nicer environment.

'My house is on a quiet, big street. You can see fields and a bus stop. Up the street is a church and bungalows for old people. It's a bad area as there is nothing to do. A good area is where you have something to do, somewhere to walk. So we just hang around on the streets. We might drink on Friday or Saturday, but there's nothing else to do. It gives the area a bad reputation. They're doing it younger and younger and it should change. I think they should build a swimming-pool or something for teenagers to get healthy. My uncle would agree with me that it's changed because teenagers are getting a lot more cocky. I think my experience is typical of other parts of the UK. Teenagers don't always find things to do. Everyone here is the same background. We all have problems, but most solve it by drinking on Friday and Saturday. I love having all my mates and family around me. It's really important to me. They are everything. If I had to choose between them and something else, I'd choose them.

'I'm thinking that if I don't buck up my ideas I won't get my GCSEs and that means no job, no life really. In Year 7 and 8, I would disagree with teachers, whatever they said, I'd bunk off lessons. I did it because everyone else around me was doing it. I did it to get sent out. In Science I'd like flick pieces of paper and Sir would send me out and I'd come back and start again and then get sent to isolation where you can't talk and all you do is work in silence. It's boring and there's nothing to do. The teacher there would tell me about his work in prison so we'd maybe think that it could be us. I don't want to be the one doing nothing in my family, no GCSEs. I'd probably be very upset and I'd have no money at all. I now don't answer back as much. I stay in lessons. It isn't easy, but you have to do it if you want to achieve. It's really hard.'

Saad

'My friends mess around and they might drive me backwards. They say things like "great you've got the grades", but when they don't get the grades they turn, it's jealousy, it's a human thing. You have got to have good friends. You can be cool and intelligent and fit in with both. You don't just have to be a geek. You have to be open and confident too. The ones who just sit at home and read books aren't going to get anywhere. You have to go that extra mile.

'My family has always put education above all else. Some families are more lenient when it comes to rules. My family always try and get me money for school trips and books.'

Katie

'A teacher should be creative and hands-on, and make you remember things. It's about attitude with some pupils, some don't have the attitude. They aspire to just getting by and not to higher things and it's not necessarily that we are going to get those higher things, but it's more likely if we want them more. Teachers generally say "do as best you can" and then I can hear pupils saying "but what if that is a fail". I think some students just don't approach teachers, but I do. Somehow teachers need to engage everyone in the school. If I could change anything it would be that "can't do it", "can't be bothered" attitude. The peer pressure too. You should just be yourself. I think there is pressure from society as well, teenagers have a bad reputation. I worry about my results, future exams and getting into university, and that teenager reputation.'

Alice, Teacher

'The main shock for me now, after a first year of teaching, is the discrepancy in standards. There are huge differences in ability levels. There are students leaving Year 11 not being able to count. The other problem is that you can rarely just teach without having to deal with behavioural issues. That can be demoralising and frustrating. It's a lack of listening and there is a lot of answering back and some of the pupils struggle to get motivated and work. There are lots of basic problems such as language barriers too, but British-born children don't have that excuse. This is a mixed school and it's interesting to see the difference in parental involvement. Many students with Asian backgrounds have more discipline at home. For some of the other students, there is no support or the parents don't necessarily get the point of education. There is a lack of enjoyment in learning and a lack of awareness of the world beyond Coventry. More Asian-background students have that awareness of the wider world. There is also the issue of classroom size. I have one class of 32 pupils and one of 30 and one of 27 and another of 22, and one of only 13. Over 30 is too much and I think that if class sizes were less than 25 that would solve some problems.'

Sam, Teacher

'As an English teacher, I use the world of words, of literature and poetry. In Barnsley, Maths is seen as solid, while English suffers from a kind of anti-masculine prejudice. Many of the pupils' fathers struggled with English themselves and the suspicion has lingered. Add to that the fact that English and literature dwell a bit too much on raw emotions and human weakness, and creativity is treated with disdain. The result is a clear problem. There is even a sort of local male pride in being bad at English. As a consequence only girls generally get through to the top English sets.

'My goal is now to engage boys with English and I've done this through poetry, particularly the poets of the First World War, and by trying to link the subject to local culture. For a while I was the only young male English teacher in the school. It was a lonely battle.'

Katie, Teacher

'Every few weeks I take time off the curriculum and we have a discussion with the pupils. I ask their opinions on books and other subjects. I don't necessarily reach into their personal lives, but I ask them for their opinions. I know that often, at home, they are not asked these things. From books we have amazing discussions on subjects such as injustice and racism. Kids from my school come from all over London, from Streatham, Peckham and Islington. It's a mixed community and many have single-parent families and very complicated lives.

'You need goals to pull you forward. Aspiration and inspiration are part of the same thing. School should be about empowerment as much as skills.'

Sarah, Teacher

'Last year I was working in an office and I realised that every time I was talking I wasn't working. I had a really good education myself and I wanted to do something more interesting than selling things for a company. Altruism and stimulation motivated me. I trained with Teach First and I came away with more ideas, with a lot to focus on. There is a responsibility. No-one else is going to do it. For many children you are the connecting thread to the outside world and culture. You realise this when a child tells you with great excitement that they've been to a restaurant for the first time. Sometimes their world is incredibly restricted. Some of my Year 10 didn't know what the word 'clergy' meant. For me educational disadvantage is disenfranchisement, there is no sense of anything for them to buy into. You try and widen their horizons, but they feel that they have no power or place in the current set-up of society.'

Alice, Teacher

'I set up a Philosophical Society during lunchtime. We started with only four or five pupils. It has expanded from just Sixth Form to include Year 8 students too. They used to hang around outside in the corridor and I got them to join in. At one stage we were 22 kids. It is the difficult Year 8 students who love to challenge me on debates. The club has become a sort of avenue for developing social skills as well as debating and discussing. We were talking about rules in society, and if and when you can make your own rules and what society expects of you, and one 13-year-old girl felt her parents should have no say in her life and we talked about when are you allowed to be an adult and why the age of eighteen is a turning point. Some students don't see that they are still children – and that attitude, I think, depends a lot on parents. Some of the most challenging students are those who don't have the home support and this 13-year-old girl finally agreed on the need for rules and we started to look at new things like the notion of things being "subjective" or "innate".

'I don't believe in lowering the level. I don't think I should be dumbing anything down. More that I should relate things to the context. For example, in R.E. I asked them to design a Facebook page for God and find links to what they knew. They wrote some really great things. One pupil, under the dimensions of God, wrote "unknown." They all have ideas, it's just unlocking them. I would like there to be more emphasis on ambition and the sense of education as a journey, as life-long, and not just putting up with five years of school.

'What skills are we developing for the future? I would like much more extra-curricular stuff. I see education as holistic and that's why I love R.E. I see education within that, and all the time furthering yourself, finding reasons, asking pupils to think about the role and purpose of humanity. Lots of them don't think like that or just fill themselves with other people's opinions.'

Josephine, Teacher

'It became obvious to me that many of the children who were going from primary level to secondary level still couldn't master reading and writing and it was having a devastating effect on their school life. Unresolved literacy issues at a young age only get worse with time. I think that many low-achieving secondary pupils only have a basic sight vocabulary of 2,000 words which enable them to scrape through, barely functioning, but scraping through all the same. These are words that they have learned to recognise and which they rehash constantly. Any new word outside their limited range cannot be deciphered, and many students go right up to a late age, and beyond, like this, with a stunted vocabulary.

'When the students are particularly disruptive or reticent in lessons, I ask them a simple question: "do you want to drive when you're older?" Generally, and without exception, they all say "yes". "For that", I say, "you need to learn to read." And the list goes on. Once the students have fully understood the stakes they tend to buckle down, perhaps comprehending inside themselves how damaged they are from the culture of not wanting to appear to try too hard.'

Ezra, Teacher

'Last year we were doing Pythagoras's theorum in 3D and to look at this, and make it more concrete, I got a pencil and a box and my first question was how big a pencil can I fit in this box and how far in? A pupil said you could try loads of different pencils and see, basically trial and error, but I said we needed precision and we only had two attempts. I had a little hand-saw and some pencils and the pupils were instantly engaged. We had studied Pythagoras in 2D, but not in 3D, and this time we were going from two to three dimensions, and we discussed methods, including algebra and square roots, and we worked it out. I'm a great believer in learning through discussion too, communicating and constructing. I encourage the students always to look at different things and take a different approach, in other words to put thinking skills into use too. I want to get them thinking differently about things and new things too, to take them further.'

Phil, Teacher

'I was a project manager for a consultancy firm in the City. I was always "chasing the dollar" as they say. The more senior I got in the company, the less and less interesting it got. I was working 80-hour weeks and all for the benefit of those higher up.

'I realised I didn't want to tell my grandchildren that I sent emails all my life. I wasn't happy working for a huge company. I wanted to get in there and start learning again. I want to inspire. I've just finished my teacher training. I know many teachers who quit the profession say that they forge their weapons for life in teaching, but I'm sort of the other way round. I came to teaching from the business world and that really helps me in my job. I see the relevance, I can see the connections between school and work. I can show them how my Maths knowledge was applied in my job.

'I'm thinking now that I would love to run a school one day. I suppose my long-term plan, if I had one, would be to become a head. I would like to have that challenge of trying to accommodate everyone from a student who was good at Maths to someone who was a musician. I suppose this dream of mine is a way of emphasising my mission and my commitment in my mind. It gets me up in the morning.'

The Earth and the Universe

by The Barbie Girls Observation

Data
Light moves fast and could travel the length of Britain in just 6 millionths of a second. At 300,000 Km/s, light from the Sun takes just over 8 minutes to reach Earth.

Debate
A guy called Shapley and a guy called Curtis had heated arguments but didn't have enough evidence to come up with a complete conclusion. Shapley suggested that we were a part of the Milky Way. However Curtis claimed that the Spiral Nebulae are Star Systems outside the Milky Way. Shapley came off better as his evidence was stronger. However a few years later the argument settled by new evidence. Curtis was right.

Lack of Evidence
'So far there is no evidence of life else where.' The great debate there were heated argument, but not enough evidence to reach an agreed conclusion.

Key words

UNIVERSE
All things (including the earth and everything else in space)

DATA!
At 300,000 Kmps light from the Sun takes just over 5 minutes to reach earth. This means that you can see sun as it was 5 minutes ago. The diameter of the milky way is 100000 light years.

Explanations

NASA began a search for extra-terrestrial intelligence. It looks for radio signals that might be produced by aliens, checking one star at a time.

Observations
Edwin Hubble used a new telescope to try to find that new far away andromeda. It seemed that andromeda, was a million light years away.

Arguments OR Conflicts
Arguments
Some nebula have a spiral shape, one of these is called andromeda. Some astronomers thought that these were island universes.

Conflicts

Evidence OR Lack of Evidence
Evidence
Harlow Shapley was investigating faint parallel of it. He could see some nebula are clusters of stars.

Lack of Evidence
So far there is no evidence of life else where.

RIGHT
Wrong!
Harlow Shapley thought that there is not universe outside the milky way. He was later proved wrong.

Team Galaxy

Gre
Water vapour
Met

Evidence

Observations
Star Distance

Observing the stars

Arguments
Some nebulae have a spiral shape, one of these is called Andromeda. Some astronomers thought that these were 'island universes' outside the milky way. There were heated 'Arguments', but not enough evidence to reach an agreed conclusion. Harlow shapley suggested that they were part of the Milky Way. Perhaps they were gas clouds. In 1920, he took part in a public debate in Washington. It was a head-to-head discussion with Heber D Curtis, another astronomer. Curtis claimed that spiral nebulae are star systems outside the milky way, they called it 'the great debate'. In the night, Shapley came off better. His evidence seemed stronger. A few years later the argument was finally settled by new evidence. Curtis had been right.

Galaxy
A collection of thousands of millions of stars held together by gravity.

Are we alone?
X-men.

Data:
- In good conditions, you can see more than 2000 stars at one time.
- At 300,000 m/s light from the Sun takes 8 minutes to reach earth.
- Parallax measurement shows that it is 4.22 light-years away (solar system)

Observations;
- Light moves through the length of Britain in just 8 millionths of a second! - Right

Explanations;
- This means you see the sun as it was 8 minutes ago.

Arguments + conflicts;
- Some astronomers thought that these 'andromeda' were 'island universe', outside the milky way. There were heated arguments.

Evidence;
- Proxima Centauri is not bright enough to see without a telescope. But

Lack of evidence;
Harlow shapley suggested that they were part of

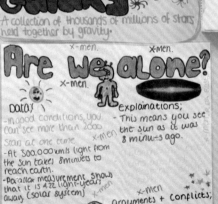

Data

Science

Explanation

Star Life Cycle!
All stars have a beginning and an end. Physical processes in a star and it's appearance throughout its life.

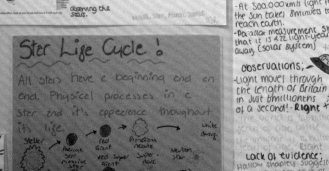

stellar nebula → red giant / red super giant → protostar nebula / super nova → white dwarf / neutron star

---

Geothermal Renewable Ba

Heat from earths crust

GROWING BUSINESS

is used to

Mark, Teacher

'I always wanted to be a policeman and kind of fell into being a teacher. I like pushing myself. I could not have a boring day job. I couldn't work in an office. This is my first year as a newly qualified teacher and I haven't been bored once. I didn't have a brilliant education myself. I have Attention Deficit Disorder (ADD) and I had to get taught by my Mum in the end. I felt let down by teachers. Having ADD made me realise how important relationships with teachers are within a school and I want to develop that. I'm able to build relationships and see where difficulties are. I have a child with special needs in Year 7, he also has ADD. I can hear him murmuring in class, without focusing. I have been able to spot his needs and I do my best to get him back on track and on the topic. I suppose I have brought more specific attention to his issues. It's easy to take for granted that we have high expectations of the students, but when you look at their background you realise that it is deprived and that there is little access to a lot of things. Often they are single-parent families and the parent just backs the kid if there is a problem or they say they are just like that. One boy was always rude to girls and when the mother was challenged, she said that he was like that at home too.

'You start in Year 7 trying to work on poor behaviour issues. There is a lack of belief. The school can help a lot. The kids I teach are not lacking, but they are not pushed or made to believe that they can succeed. We have to get rid of that belief that they can't achieve, especially those from families where education doesn't mean anything to them.'

Anna, Teacher

'It is maybe old-fashioned, but I believe that there is a problem when pupils talk about teachers earning their respect. Perhaps it should be the other way round? I know it's a bit of a stereotype to place blame with parents when talking about some of the issues surrounding educational disadvantage, but there can often be a clash when parents transmit their own negative experiences of school and their own attitudes vis-a-vis authority. There are those parents who tell their children that you should respect adults and those who tell their offspring that adults, particularly teachers, have to earn your respect. This difference of attitude is a serious matter, a dangerous one even.

'I see children who have an inflated sense of entitlement, who believe they have an innate right to be critical of teaching staff – and that is undoubtedly a challenge. Getting pupils on side is a major aim of my work at the school. It adds a dynamic to my tasks as a teacher. Every day in which the relationship between a pupil and teacher grows is progress. My continuous three-year stint at the school has been a huge plus in my contact with pupils, especially in an inner-city school like this where the staff turnover is high. It takes time to build trust and personal relationships with pupils, let alone parents.

'Discipline is a complex issue for every child and evolves according to the age group. I have one pupil who has been challenging on a continual basis because his own father left school without qualifications and with some resentment, and a gripe against teachers. The boy has an issue with boundaries, but he now knows what I tolerate and what I won't tolerate from his personality. When I first started as a teacher, I followed the rule book and then came to see that the way to do it is to build relationships with students over time, individually, one by one.'

Liam

'Something just happens, too, you grow up and you click. You think, right you've got six months, what can I do with it? That's all I had left to put my head down. I wish I'd put more effort into it, into learning and then I'd have got out of school much better. But I'm lucky to be here. I'm 16 and I'm getting paid to work, so ... not many kids have got these kind of opportunities have they?

'I didn't ever think I'd see myself sat here in this seat right now (as the school caretaker). All I wanted to do was go to college, go to work with my Dad because he's a manager of a gasket company. But, you know, things change don't they? Every day, every minute, every second of the day things change. Working here, it's a good feeling. I love it. Just yesterday they gave me the alarm code for the building. They must have trust in you so you don't go blurt it out to kids and I've got every key to this building nearly, except one office. When you're a student you think, ah it's easy being a teacher and all this. But you get kids talking to you like you're not there and stuff. It was a surprise really that one minute you're being naughty, the next you're telling people off.'

The Perfect Teacher

- have children calm
- Give children for things
- like have to be funny
- they funny to remarks
- Make at their job
- smart
- NO RACISM
- Give Merits alot and
- Postcards
- No Demerit

Mr one

helped me

Workshop VI:
What makes the perfect teacher ...?

Writing exercises about ideal teachers, homework, or what constitutes a good education, were particularly instructive. Teachers wanted pupils to have a free rein and not feel inhibited – and would sometimes leave the room during writing workshops. It was extremely rare, however, for a pupil to use our writing exercises to denigrate a specific teacher. Instead, students described the roles teachers played in 'turning them round' prior to exams or how they managed to make them 'step back from the brink' over a disciplinary issue. Many pupils, too, said they only liked Maths or English because of certain teachers. Some even wanted to become teachers in later life because they could see the nurturing influence their own teachers had had on them.

Teachers were willing to go the extra mile for their pupils, but they were also mindful that they could not replace a family or community structure around a child. It is alarming, some noted, that a 'good teacher' is, in some circles, seen as someone who has to be a multitasking superhero, making up for the failures and dysfunctions of wider society.

Difficult situations led teachers to create their own conditions for change, completely revamping their subjects to make them more active and dynamic, fund-raising for school trips, setting up clubs for cooking, philosophy, film and creative writing: creating their own opportunities to make the transformations they knew were needed.

Laughs !
and interacts
with the
Class

A major
inspiration

Should give
you a good
education

Lessons are
very interactive

Ideal
teacher

Speaks quite
loud (engaging

Keeps the points
straight forward

Support
given when
needed

A good
friend !

What makes the perfect teacher ...?

When you learn to be smart and nice and a good person. Also you learn all the bits of life like making friends and how to not be a loner and to like be yourself and be kind.

A good education is an education that sets you up for the challenges of life.

Education gives us an understanding of how life works. We might not think that it is useful now, but in the end it will all pay off and we will be so happy that we didn't give up so early in life when we could be having all these wonderful things which life has rewarded us with.

When you are happy to be learning and not bored to learn. It is when the teachers are enthusiastic and kind and don't give you warnings or detentions.

When you known everything that lies ahead of you. So you understand everything that is to be asked of you in your future. This education would also allow you to do or be anything you want in life.

Where you learn useful things that will help you achieve in life. For a good education, teachers should engage you and make lessons fun and interesting, so you can remember what you have learned. As well as having fun, everyone should be kept under control. You should learn everything you need for the future and you should always be improving so you become a well-rounded person.

Chapter 8
Afterword: Six Months On

We were careful when interviewing people for this book not to put official permissions forms in front of them just as conversations were getting underway. We didn't want anyone to feel inhibited and opinions had to come to the surface naturally, within their right context. This approach, however, meant that once we had put the book together we had the hard task of contacting our contributors all over again.

It has been fascinating, six months on from the interviews, to go back to the people we interviewed and gauge their reactions to their own words. It has enabled some to consider their opinions objectively, and in writing, for the first time. For others, it has allowed them to see how much their lives have changed since they were interviewed. Six months is quite a short amount of time, but it is indicative of the fragility of some students' lives that a mere half-year has led to dramatic changes in several cases. In one city, in the Midlands, we were initially unable to track down a young woman because her father, with whom she lived, had been evicted. She had had to move in with her mother again and that was exactly the situation she had wanted to avoid.

Such instability was witnessed with another pupil who had been to-ing and fro-ing between parents before getting in trouble with the police in his area in the North East. He was hard to locate and his non-attendance at school had become a problem. In fact, we were told his position in the institution was looking increasingly untenable.

Roberta, the youth club worker from Byker in Newcastle upon Tyne, stood by all that she said, even though she deplored the fact that her words about her neighbourhood could potentially be construed as negative. She loved her area, but she knew she couldn't be blinkered about its problems. Another permission for a photo was turned down by a protective London grandmother because she didn't want her granddaughter to be distracted during her exam period, even for a positive reason like a photo in a publication. Such sacrifices are necessary, the grandmother noted, when the odds are piled against you.

Changes have been positive for many contributors too and, here again, the role of supportive teaching was fundamentally brought home. One student had won a short story award thanks to the encouragement and insistence of his English teacher. Another pupil had managed to turn his behaviour around and the school no longer had to call the boy's parents twice a week. A teacher, who had been particularly vocal about the need for teaching staff to engage in their own research, described how she was now taking up the challenge of pursuing her own studies alongside her work.

And it was not just teachers who had undergone these alterations in their thinking. It seemed to us, as originators of this book, that we, too, had experienced some fundamental shifts in our ideas and awareness. The ever-escalating insecurity of deprivation had really hit home. Just as educational disadvantage is not one thing, but a conglomerate of connected issues, so it cannot be frozen in time. With every day that passes it is either mitigated in some way or it begins spiralling even more out of control. A student who is in a situation of precariousness can easily tip over the edge and that tipping point can be anything from a parent or relative moving out, to the departure of a supportive teacher or an unforeseen expenditure. It is then that the fragile edifice of a school career collapses or teeters dangerously on the brink. And just as the pendulum of chance and experience can swing towards advantage it can rush backwards too. It is not an understatement to say that a child in a situation of disadvantage can have his or her world turned upside down at the drop of a hat.

With that threat in the background, it felt all the more reassuring and hopeful to hear teachers say 'that is truly what I believe' or 'I stick by that' as they signed their permissions forms.

About the Authors

Greg Villalobos wanted to be a marine archaeologist when he was younger. As it turns out, he paid far more attention in his Art classes than History and decided to pursue a career in the creative industries. He has spent over a decade working with young people at the fringes of mainstream society. He holds true to the belief that stories have the ability to captivate, inspire, promote action and ultimately create change. In 2004 he co-founded Bold Creative, a digital agency that helps organisations campaign with and on behalf of the young people they serve, winning numerous awards in the process. In 2009 he married a Teach First Ambassador and started a long running relationship with the charity, contributing to numerous campaigns. He now lives in Northumberland.

www.gregvillalobos.co.uk

Ben Faccini spent several years working in education for a United Nations agency before dedicating himself to writing novels and non-fiction. Following on from his experiences at the United Nations, he has written extensively on issues in the developing world, particularly on street children, working children and innovations in education. He is writer-in-residence at a London school for First Story, a charity which fosters literacy and creativity in young people from 'schools in challenging circumstances. Since 2010 he has been involved in several initiatives to train teachers in creative-writing skills. He lives in London.

Interviews: Greg Villalobos and Ben Faccini
Workshops and Writing: Ben Faccini
Photos and Design: Greg Villalobos

Greg and Ben with Ayanle, London

Thank You

The publication of this book would not have been possible without the contribution of hundreds of young people, parents and teachers across the UK. In particular, we wish to extend our warmest thanks to staff and pupils at the following:

Bethnal Green Academy, London

Burlington Danes Academy, London

Barrs Hill School and Community College, Coventry

Cranford Community College, London

The Dearne Advanced Learning Centre, Yorkshire

Freebrough Academy, West Yorkshire

Hallfield Primary School, London

Harborne Academy, Birmingham

Holland Park School, London

Queens Park Community School, London

YMCA Byker, Newcastle upon Tyne

The community of Byker, Newcastle upon Tyne

We are also indebted to First Story for their support with the writing workshops. (First Story fosters creativity, literacy and talent in secondary schools.)

For more information about this publication and the work of Teach First in helping every child succeed, regardless of their background, please visit teachfirst.org.uk

Registered charity no.1098294